Mull:

A Poem a Day Keeps the Thoughts at Bay

Joram *Nampi*

Presentation by *BookLeaf Publishing*

Web: www.bookleafpub.com

E-mail: info@bookleafpub.com

ISBN: 9789363305212

First edition 2024

Immersion

Let my soul drift
    in streams of words;
Let my body sink
    in pools of sentences.

So when I die,
I'll become a part of it.
And when someone sees it,
They'll find me
    underneath.

Alchemy

Tiny,
itsy-bitsy pieces of words,
Sewn
together to create
sentences;
Inked with emotions
To let the readers
Feel
the
words
In poetry.

Call it magic!
But
poems are feelings,
Perceived
Through
words.

Essence

Mere words and mere thoughts,
Rhymes—
The mere poetry.

Inspiration

Read poetry
To
Emit poetry.

MANIFEST

5

<pre>
                My eyes still numb
          Whenever I write;
     Tapping into my deepest conscience,
          I pluck out a few thoughts
                     And embellish them
with the name of

          Poetry.
</pre>

Echoes

A while since I had gone back
to my thoughts,

And today when I closed
my eyes for a moment,

The freshly departed fragments
of those abandoned musings
waved through my mind.

However, it felt soothing,
And just for today,
Maybe,
Let it
caress me
once more.

Reflections

From work to home,
I really enjoy those silent strolls;

Walking alone, listening to
the nearby noises,

Deciphering nature
amidst the hustle,
While my mind ponders
Over questions
Left
unanswered.

Nostalgia

Once, if possible,
I'd like to sit on a bench
Somewhere,

Reminiscing all those days
of yore that I'd lived,

Quietly crooning
the songs that incited
My soul,

In solitude
or maybe not.
Who knows?

Though someday,
Certainly,
If possible.

Imprints

The memories etched on my mind
will linger for quite a while,

Though I may never know
for how long
they'll stay.

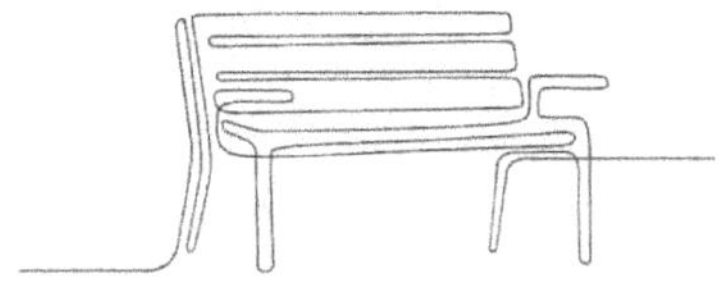

Ephemera

The goal of living
is
to live
without regrets
until
we dissipate
into
nothing
but memories

SUBLIME

Beauty, so great!
So divine;
Numbing me to the extent
That I fail
to grasp it in mere words.

The moon, full of itself,
Shines like a lamp in the night.
Barks—
The silent breeze strokes the
leaves;
A sudden, excited dog licks me,
While all I can do
is
write.

Tranquil

Twinkling starlight up above,
And the crescent moon upon us;

How such a peaceful night can be so
kindred!
Sitting on the man-made
concrete,
I look up towards them,
Calmly letting the fluent sight
of it
Within me.

Respite

Gazing at those trees, their leaves
caressed by the silent autumn
breeze,

perhaps,
destiny can wait
for a bit.

Mirage

Let this breeze
carry these thoughts
far away to somewhere,
In a far-off land.

And from there,
let them be what they are,
merely,
a mirage.

Serenity

Those green hues I'm looking at,
The wind breezing through my body
As it signals the beginning of
fall.

Mellifluous and soothing.

Lectures and whispered voices
Fade into the background.
A warm blush tingles my cheeks;
Giddiness stirs in my stomach.
These sudden emotions
swirl all around.
With a halt, the class ends.
And I leave,
abruptly.

Surrender

Calm yourself
a bit
And
Let the world
flow
within you.

Bliss

What should I write about now?
The philosophies that reside within
Or the beautiful past I made
With the world.

It's purely blissful
to write about everything
And yet
Know nothing.

Divine

Such sublimity,
A euphonious symphony.
Innumerable writings could be
penned
From its sound.
An inspiration, its nobility.

So young I am,
Yet
Seeing this feels as if these eyes have
witnessed
the entirety of existence.
My essence fulfilled,
My soul, content.
Such beauty.

Sanctuary

Fly, my tears,
        To unseen dimensions
           Where none can grasp
The truth of my soul

Paradox

How time flies
And how it stays still
All at the same time.

How clouds move
Yet seem still
All at once.

A bit of patience,
And little by little,
Everything shifts
by itself.

Time

No ends,
No intervals.
Time was there
when nobody was.
Time is what we have,
Within ourselves,
And
Everywhere around us.

Continuum

24

We shall not perish,
For we are the universe,
Living within itself.

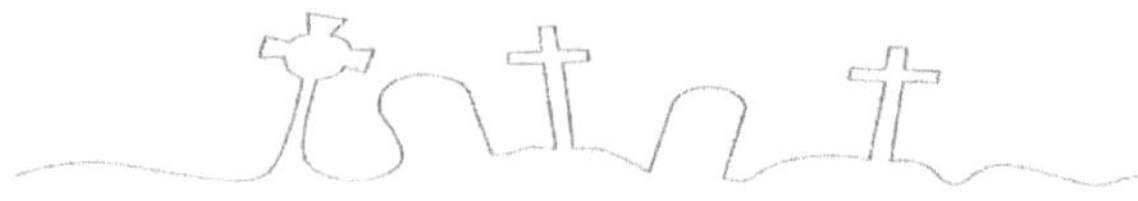

Eternal

Merging with the universe,
Living within everything,
May my soul not be reborn,
Even if my existence ceases forever;
Let me melt
Into eternal bliss,
Peacefully.

Yearning

In all this chaos running amok:
The demeaning words,
The lesser hopes,
Just a little more peace
My soul yearns for;

And with eyes all teary-blurred,
While every muscle turns numb,
Just a little more time,
My mind longs for.

Melancholy

Melancholy miseries
    all around,
       Gloomy thoughts
         go round and round,
           Stealthily,
      they find their way
    Into monotony,
day by day.

         Melancholic days
     stretch
   on and on,
   Melancholy
      miseries
        all around.

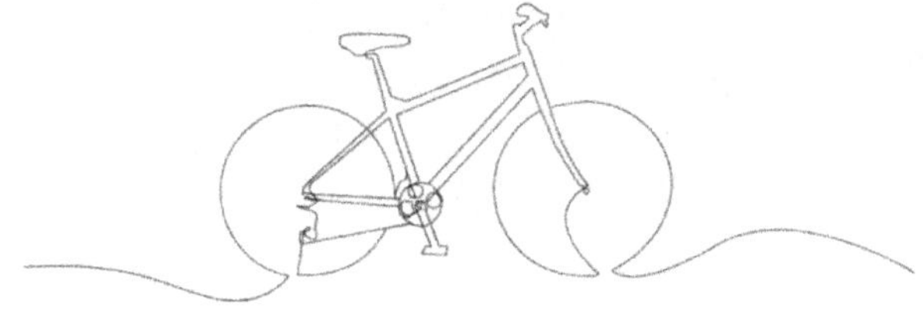

Inevitable

In the face of imminent death,
Nothing will remain,
And surely,
we will cease
To exist.

Desolation

The lingering smoke
        Hangs in the air,
So sad, so horrifying—
        The night had no stars.

A pleasant afternoon
        Gave rise to a terrifying disaster
        That no one predicted.

    As the flames faded,
        The weight of loss set in.
    Amidst it all
Lay the grim moods of people,
        Mourning the loss of everything
            they had,
Reduced to ashes
        By a mere flicker of a spark.

    And now, all they have left
        Is nothing.

Upheaval

In mere seconds,
everything changed;
Who bears the blame?
The people fighting for their rights,
Or the soldiers bound by duty?
Firearms crackled,
protesters roared,
Igniting a war among humans.
But beneath it all,
lies the hidden game of politics,
And now, humanity lies shattered.

Expression

In quiet moments of serenity,
The words come overflowing.
Is it a gift,
  Or a curse—
The ability to jot down
My emotions
Into words?

Writing

33

Writing,
an integral part of me,
never fails.
Even in my most flawed verses,
I found my greatest lessons.

Fragments

Words flow on their own,
        Yet nothing comes to fruition
    When I try to lay down
        The depths of my thoughts.

A few sentences, here and there,
        Stumble through my mind,
So I wrote them
        In these lines.

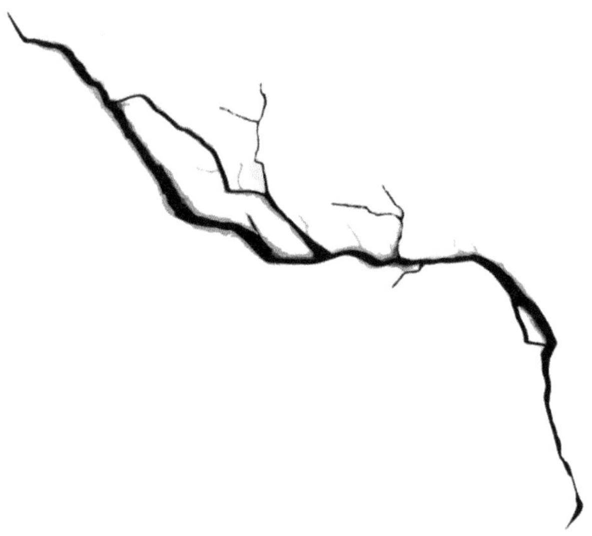

Unwritten

All gone,

        My thoughts, all gone;
My words, all gone.

          It feels so numb,
Not scribbling for so long,
           Weak, helpless.
My mind is a blank slate,
        Empty.

Why can't I weave these thoughts?
        They drift like teasing winds;
Running to and fro,
Yet, I couldn't sew my thoughts
        Into a few words.

Transience

Fleeting
          memories,
Fleeting
                    passersby,
          and
Fleeting
                    thoughts.

Chaos

My mind shattered into pieces.
Heavy thoughts, fractured reasoning,
Delusions racing through my mind.
I wish to control it,
But why is it so hard to contain?
Bound in chains of
senseless mysticism,
And the beast is
unleashed.
Consequences,
many.
Salvation,
none.

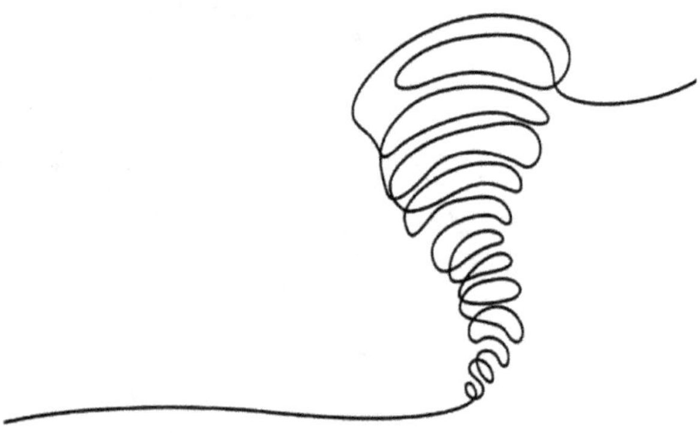

Faded

My mouth no longer speaks
                    the words it once
                              knew,
My hands
no longer   write
as they
                                        did,
And my
              thoughts
no long
      er

                  ma
                    ke

              s
              e
            nse.

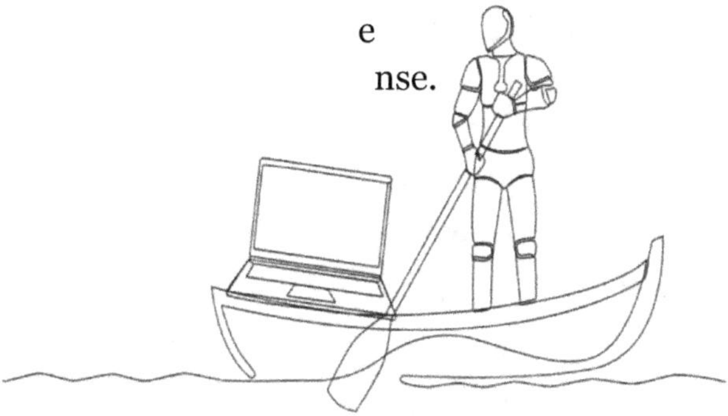

Insecurities

Hydrophobia: the fear of water.
Though my body longed to
submerge
Within
these
undulating
waters,
My mind
resisted.
A fear,
you see;

A phobia of merging with the waves,
Relinquishing control,
Allowing the
shifting tides
to take over.
The fear
reminded me
Of my own insecurities.

Sitting by the rocks,
I looked at my fear,
Anxiously.

Desirer

Drenching myself
in a vicious lust
for another,
Ruining my soul
with selfish yearnings,
Fiddling with innocence
in my perverse thoughts—

How grievous!

Forbidden

Oh!
When will it end?
These forbidden thoughts.
Restraining my sanity, my consciousness.
Restless nights—
Forsooth!

A
  soaring
      pleasure
         until
            it
              peaks,
              A
        disrupting
      guilt
     when
   it
descends.

                  Alas! I lay down,
                  Confined in regret.

Unspoken

<pre>
            Sometimes
    I want   to vent
my   thoughts,
    Not   through
      simple   words
          But   in
              letters
                  spoken
                      aloud.
</pre>

Void

A blink!

And
my
vision

    fades;

My thoughts

run away from me,
  And I follow them
  into oblivion,

Only to land in my own emptiness.

Nocturnal

Sleep!

Was I so cruel
that
you've
left me to rot?

A myriad of thoughts
flowed
through my
restless mind—
Neither could I think

Nor rest in these
peaceful
arms of my bed.

Ah!

The owl's totem pecked me.
As I lay down
With my eyes wide open.
'Nocturnal,'
My wicked mind murmured.

Illusion

48

For a while, my thoughts were all fogged up.
Though looking at the bigger picture,
I realized how idiotic I was—

Treating

minute details

as if they were monumental.
How foolish, indeed.

Awakening

The sudden **reveal**
of reality—
And
for a moment,
I thought
It was
all
a dream.

Jabber

Jumbled my words are,
all in dismay

Now,
Yabbers in

Awe!

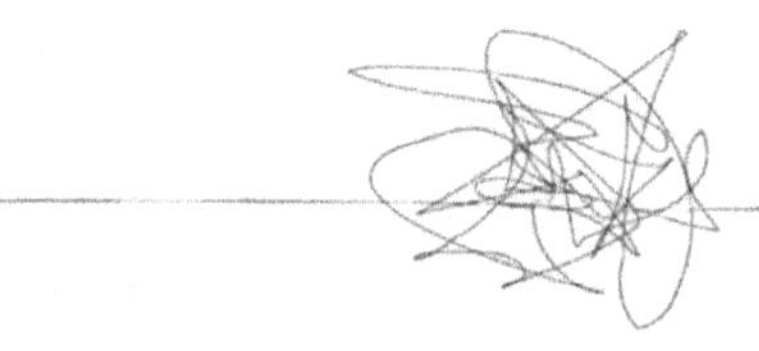

Conundrum

I do not know to whom
my thoughts belong:

A mere human

or

The World?

Moment

That peaceful day, I still remember——
*The sun's rays dimming behind distant
mountains,*
And the trees quietly shedding their leaves
As the melodies of saints flowed through
my ears,
My mind
And my soul.

**In that moment, I realized the meaning of
peace—**
It's beautiful.

Doze

The softness of my bed,

The warmth of my room—

My peaceful little heaven.

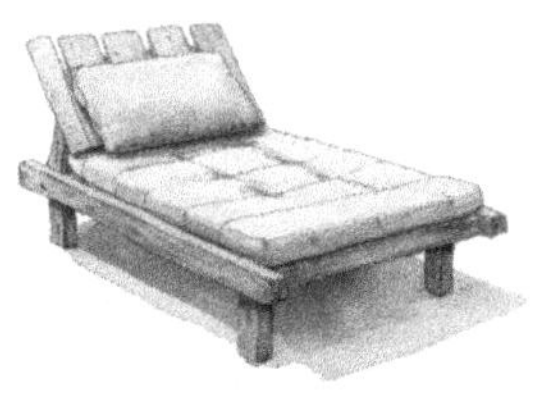

Feminine

54

*My words **weave an elegance***
As my soul spills itself into a poem.
My thoughts, delicate,
Unlike the sharpness of my actions.
And so, my essence is etched
*In the soft glow of **pure ecstasy**.*

Thoughts

Do they even care about the sentences you're trying to convey?
Do they ever reminisce or inquire about the subjects you discuss?
Do they only pity themselves?
Like I'm doing right now.

Pause

Silence all around—

Or maybe not.

Is the whole world in silence?

Or is it my thoughts

at peace?

Persistence

What once was a dream
Is now my reality.
>But

>>Am I happy?

It's a strong word.

There are still ups and downs,
Yet they seem minor now.
>Though I strive for more,
>I find peace in what I have,
>In what I've felt,

>And in what I've written.

Clarity

There's noise all around,

But when attuned to one's thoughts,

The chaos starts to

d
i
s
s
i
p
a
t
e

Seasons

I'm still writing for the beauty that resides
Within everything:

      The c a l m of spring
         Leading to summer's
        ***warmth*,**
           Those sprinkling
           monsoon
         o e r
     h   w
  s   s
That soothe the rough lands,
    And autumn's radiant colors

Ushering in winter's chill.

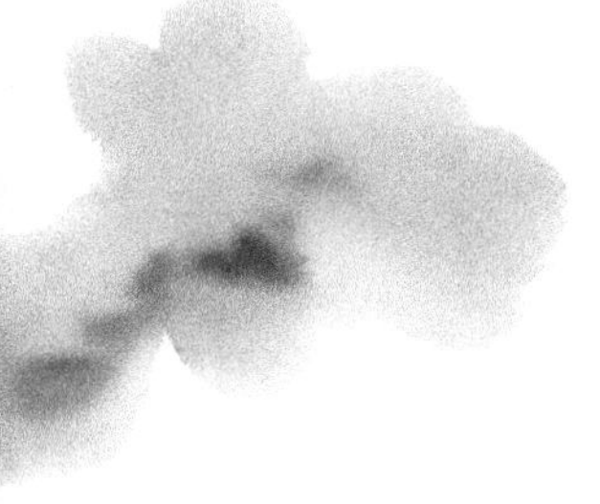

Elusive

A few thoughts l a   n g up above,
              f o ti
'Which one to write?'
My mind wondered.
Poof!
There they go—
My c h a i n
                  o f
                        t
                          h
                            o
                            u
                            g
                            h
                            t

Phantoms

Why, brain,
    Did you conjure up these en d l   e s   s
                    dreams,
These unfulfilled wishes,
        None of them, real?
A sudden jolt struck me,
And its effect,
        Long-lasting.

Escape

The heavy
traffic,
the
heat's s
But   w
with   e
a   a
simple   t
pair
of
earbuds,
The world
transforms into
something
More   surreal,
More   pleasant,
More blissful.

Drained

Weary of these endless thoughts,
Exhausted all day long.
I rest beneath the weight of my writings,
Still,
I'm drained.
    So tired,
        Of myself.

Now

Neither
the past
Nor
the future—
I write solely
For the present.

Rush

No moon, no stars,
As clouds thickened overhead.
Thundering roars echoed through the sky,
A breeze arrived, carrying a thrill toward
us.
Raindrops kissed our faces, cooling our
thirst.
We waited no longer—
We dashed into the storm,
Without umbrellas, embracing the rain.

Resilience

Alone,
In a foreign land,
With no words to share,
Yet thousands of thoughts to bear.
How will they express them?
How will they reveal themselves?
In a place where they find no kin,
No one of their own.
Still,
A flicker of hope remains,
For
They believe in themselves.
Alone,
Yet
Unyielding.

Discrete

The woven words,
     my quiet language.
The unseen writings,
     a guarded secret.
The silent voices,
     forever hidden.

Secrets

The vast secrets within—
All useless!
They'll fade to nothing,
soon enough.

Reverie

These memories I cherish,

of days long past,

Those dreams that offer glimpses

of the uncharted future,

But for now,

This solitude is enough.

Repetition

The seasons

repeat　　　their

endless　　　　　　cycle,

The　　　　　　　　monotony

of　　　　　　　　　life,

always　　　　the same.

Should I act?

But

What can I do?

This endless loop

leaves me　　　　　hollow,

Caught　　　　　　in chains,

But are　　　　　they real?

Or just　　　obstacles

of my own creation?

Scribbles

With scattered thoughts and restless words,
I scribble frantically, all around.
Across roughened pages with blue ink,

The pen trembles in my fidgeting hands.
'Sleep,' my wicked mind

whispers.

But,

'Can you?'

As the clock strikes three.

Secrecy

The blissful weather,
While emotions surge within.
So overpowering, these thoughts,
But held in quiet restraint.
Will they ever escape,

Or

Burst ^{forth} only as words?

Departure

Walk with me down this road,

And when our paths diverge,

We will bid farewell;

Merrily remembering

Each other in memories.

Everyone must depart someday

So why not end it joyfully?

Peace

In the end,

We only look for one thing.

Peace,

Within ourselves.

Home

Let's walk together
Through this life,
Discovering the mysteries
of the unknown.
Join me
In every moment,
Whether good or bad.
Together,

We'll find our home

In this vast world,

Where we'll live

For eternity.

Solitude

The moon hides behind the clouds,
Casting no light on my path,
I walk with only me
And my solitude.

It was nice—
The feeling of being alone.
Solitude, it never bothered me.

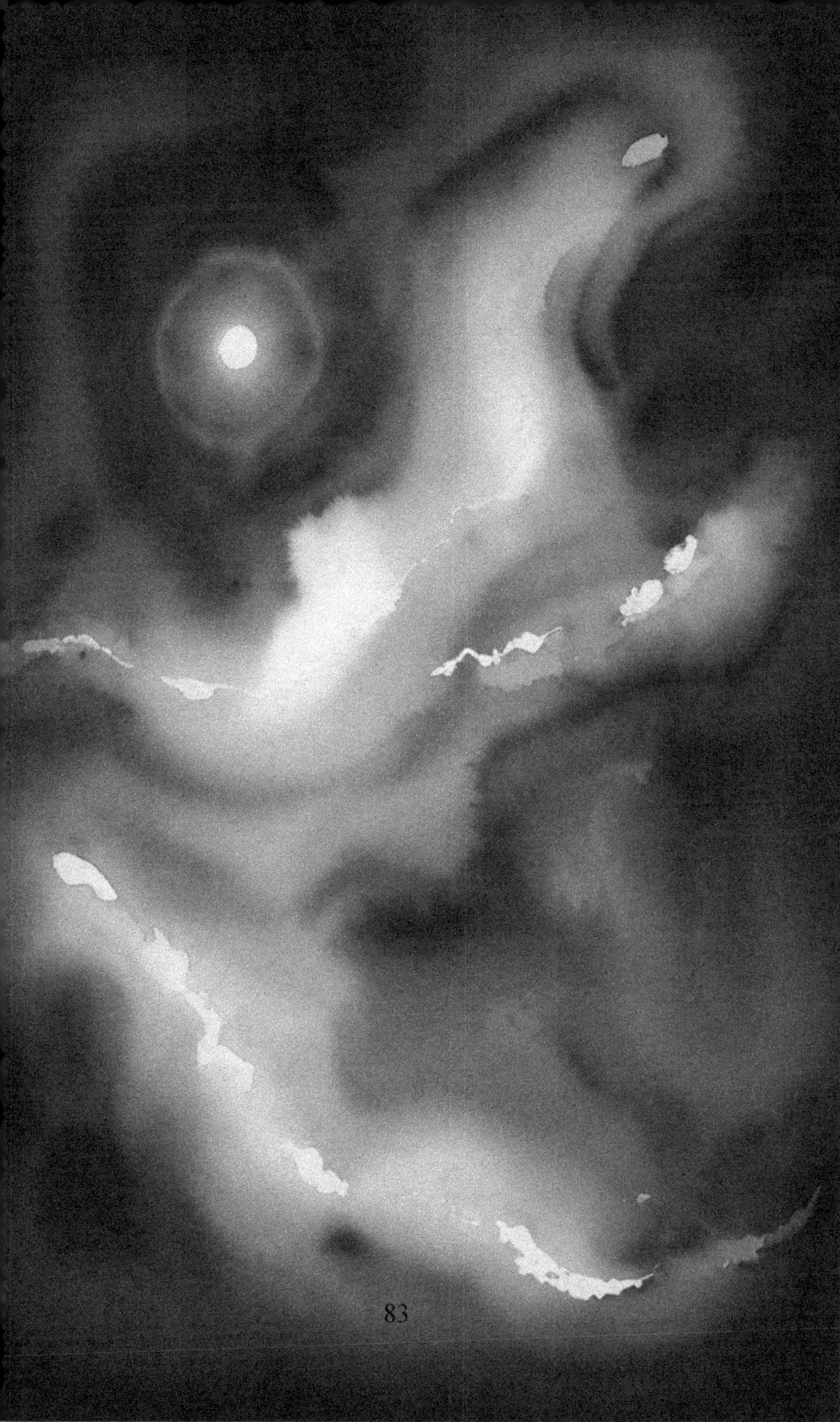

Weariness

Tired of all this,

Lying on the soft earth,

As _time_

flies

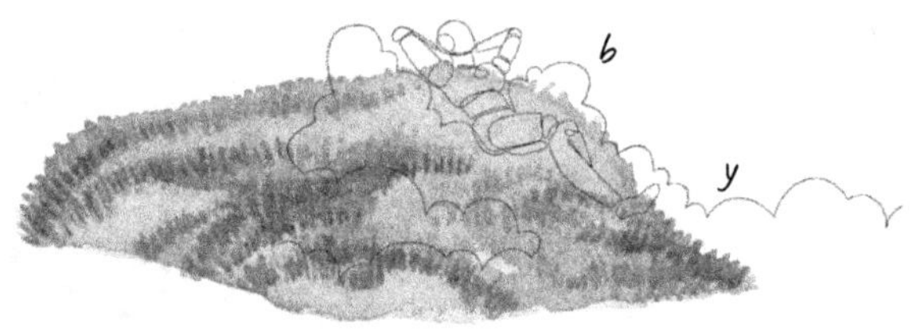

9 789363 305212